Love and Other Deaths

.

Love
and Other
Deaths

poems by D. M. Thomas

Paul Elek   London

Published in Great Britain 1975 by
Elek Books Limited
54–58 Caledonian Road, London NI 9RN

ISBN 0 236 31016 x

Acknowledgments
Grateful acknowledgments are due to the following, in
which many of the poems in this volume first appeared:
Ambit, the BBC (Poetry Now), the *Critical Quarterly*, the
Denver Quarterly, *Encounter*, the *London Magazine*, *Midland
Read*, *New Humanist*, *New Letters*, *New Worlds*, the *New
York Times*, *Poetry* (Chicago), *New Poetry 1973*, the *Poetry
Review*, *Poetry Workshop*, the Keepsake Press, the Priapus
Press, Second Aeon Publications, the *Spectator*, *The Times
Literary Supplement*, and the *Transatlantic Review*.

Printed in Great Britain by The Anchor Press Ltd
and bound by Wm Brendon & Son Ltd
both of Tiptree Essex
and set in Monotype Baskerville

Contents

Author's Note

Part I contains poems of death and loss. Part II consists of poems on a variety of themes. Most of the poems in Part III take as their starting-point a complex love relationship. Part IV is a love-sequence, having as its stage a central contemporary myth: the kidnapping of a diplomat by extremists. Part V consists of two works: a sexual-creation sequence involving Eve's apocryphal rival, Lilith; and an erotic love poem written in response to the ancient Chinese book of divination, the *I Ching* or Book of Changes.

I

Nurses

Longshoremen

What strange cargoes

what crude-packed cargoes they load or unload
with a nonchalant expertise
as though saying
there is more
there is always more

the owners calm down
shakily join in the banter
it is not life or death

whatever sent forth
white meat
delicate jewelled instruments
there is meat enough in their own larders
watches on their own wrists
held out and sustaining
the otherways-gripped load so steadily

they appear to know to the split-second
when the scarcely moving hulk
has passed in hazy water
the line of indisputable demarcation

it is good
it is all good

on the waterfront
        to smoke the good cigarette

on the water
                to be so still

Cecie

The evening that you died was the first I could not
Overhear you bed-down with your 'dear Nellie':
No farting and whispering. The house lay cursed
Not with one death only: with its own.
Who, you asked in my head, will lace my brother's
Shoes up in the morning, empty the chamberpots
And dress my sister? There was no reply.
I heard you struggle to sit up in the coffin.
You'd have worked all night and worked off that deep hurt.

Dear aunt, if Christ had come, as well he might, to you,
You'd have scrubbed his feet with good soapy water
Left from Monday's wash, pocketed a few
Fresh loaves and fishes for your poor sister;
Burnt your hand on the boiler, muttered, 'That's nothin'',
Run out, lisle stocking flapping, to dig the garden.

You demand—clucking at the grave in such a state,
From our habit of taking you for granted—shears,
Scrubbing-brush, water, not for your sake but hers
You lie beside again. An image of you: triangle:
Lawn, mower and you (no taller than it)
Leaning a force three times your fleshless weight.
70, your death shocked us like a child's.

In all but stoicism you *were* a child.
Rampaging through the village you never left,
Blackberry-faced, hot pasties in your apron,
Scuttling, chuckling. No breasts to hold or suck at.

You had no life. No lovers that I know of.
Yet we all loved you. You were filled with love
No-one repaid. Death can't be a still
Nor a cobwebbed house any longer, full of your labour,
Farting, scurrying. You have no death.
So much living is living still.

Rest-Home, Visiting Hour

Having lifted you by armpits morbidly frail,
The texture of russian cream, brushed your thin hair,
We slid our eyes off you. Moots with the dead,
Death-cells, terminal wards, agree that where
The future is taboo, love's voices fail.

My nuclear family and I
You were on the rim
Of like a cold, small, barren planet filled the room
With bright sinister terror that you would cry
Towards the end of the visit. And you did.

I switched on your transistor. The stainless-steel sill
Held snaps of our too many dead we left you
To commune with about us. Aunt, when you made
That supreme effort of your will,
Which white wall did you turn your face into?

We were too far away.
You prayed
To be taken. Day after day
The light gathered towards afternoon, and diminished,
With no interruptions from voices, until you vanished.

The Journey

Mother, hear the wind keening over the Goss Moor,
Tregeagle's sighs, emptying the bottomless Dozmare
Pool. Seeing the world again begins to bore
You. You rub seized joints. I ask you how you are
And the wind fails to force the car
Off the A30. Yes, it is good of me to drive so far,

For one almost as old and bald as Dozmare,
Her life, apart from me, featureless as Goss Moor.
I compute how far
We have to go: seven hours. She who bore
Me is pressed, small, while the decimal nines are
Flickering into noughts, back into the car,

As I was, waiting. I ask how you are;
Must I wind down the window a shade, raise the car-
Heater? It is wrinkled Tregeagle emptying the Dozmare
Pool in you, discomfort, pain, that never fall far
Before rising to the same level. Your harpings bore
Me like this incessant wind over the Goss Moor.

And I cannot look sideways in the car,
It is too painful to see how shrunken you are,
Tacitly, since last the Goss Moor
Shot past us, and hidden Dozmare;
Three thousand miles on the gauge since I came so far
To fetch you. That January day you bore

Me, did the journey feel so far?
Image of starry countdowns that move and bore
Us, I dice with the petrol countdown, see if the car
Will reach the next pump, past Bodmin Moor.
You rest trustful in my omniscience. Old Dozmare
Mother, what strange things and what strangers we are.

I know these three weeks you will bore
Me. I don't read your letters when you are far

Away, those cheerful comforting lies. So; till you are
Dead, as something wants, and, dead, I drive this car
Or the next, for the last time up through the moor
That rose when Dozmare was sea, and sees the end of
     Dozmare.

I help you struggle from the car, to a moorstone. You bore
Your own small Dozmare in thin soil. For we are water and
     moor,
And far journeyers together. Whatever else we are.

The Bridge

Taking, each of us, one of my father's hands,
Created a kind of bridge
Of his death between us.
I paid the toll, moved on, and pay it yet.

My mother is still there, upon that bridge.

I look back at it, as from some vantage,
Watch the graceful
Illuminated curves of iron,
The frozen waiting headlamps. The night.

Reticent

How they loved understatement!
'Goin' a' drop rain, are us?'—the sky
an enraged bladder. 'He've had a drop to drink.'
'I dear like bit ride'—those grotesque tea-treat safaris
to Weston-super-Mare or Timbuctoo,
with a break for drop tea and a brisk turn
round the amazement-arcades before starting back.
'Nice few taties this year, 'n?' 'Nice bit o' meat, plenty
for all of us.' 'He've got a shillin' in his purse'
—John Jago with his Johannesburg gold-shares.
'Are you goin' to kiss me? 'Cause you're goin' away
for a few minutes'—I to my Oxford term.
It expressed their landscape;
deep labyrinths under the shafted bracken.

Now a drop of rain drums on a good few graves.
Plenty enough for me.
Some with not even a jampot to catch it.
When I've had a drop to drink
I can bear my mother's lonely, painful descent;
'You're not looking too bad.'
Cursed with the style, I felt embarrassed to
bend and kiss my father's tortured face,
he 'no better' behind the corner screen,
he going away for a few minutes.
Liking bit ride, I drive 200 miles
to glance at my watch till it's time to go again.
Without exaggeration the landscape weeps.
I've got a shilling but I can't spend it.

Dream

My woman said to me
I feel so guilty
at never knowing your father

       why don't you let him
       come and fetch me on sunday
       for the big easter tea at your house
       instead of you?

              And have him come early
              then he can sleep with me
              if you don't mind

       Mind! I was very pleased and excited
       easter day parties at our house
       are terribly grim with the dead
       still in their grave clothes & still dying
       & just a cup of potato wine

When I met him from the cemetery
it was wonderful
to see him so much better & younger
so wiry & healthy &
filthy dirty from work & his carroty
hairtufts I'd forgotten
making his whole body glow like an indian brave

       but when it came to it
       I didn't like to ask him
       if he'd fetch my woman

              because he'd forgotten the letter f
              & fourteen years of death
              makes driving strange & dangerous

       it might seem I was taking advantage
       I couldn't be open with him

and he
    humble as always   reticent
    he didn't want to seem pushing

Rubble

I sit in my mother's cramped bedsit,
on edge in body and spirit.
The light too bright for her eyes.
The radio too loud for her ears.
The low fire too hot for her
seized limbs appalling me.

Yet she wants to live.
Yet to rejoin her husband.
To win, lose, tie, go on running.

Almost it is a quarter to nine
when I can jump up, heat
her milk and water, kettle
for her bottle, pull out the commode,
compel myself to kiss her, and go.

She is a fledgling
broken on the road
I want to be out of sight of.
But alive, or the world will fold.

It is as though the black hole
drawing her into itself
is conditioning my love
to require absence. She knows

it. She is content. There is
a queer radiance in the space
between us which my eyes
avoid occupying: the radium
Madame Curie found, when desolate
she returned at night to the empty table.

II

Symphony in Moscow

(homage to Rachmaninov)

        This crowd waiting patiently
    in the icy street
      these notes
        still flying in this head-
scarfed auditorium
      these tears
        turning to crystals of transistors
      on these eyelashes these cheeks

    this rain
        on faces
           frozen in too long
  a winter
      this forest without murders
these silver birches and black pines
        winging

      these silences in midflight
        the heart thrown forward
    this girl
      stepping out of the crowd
    pressing this simple orange
  into the hands of the English conductor

now in the icy street
      at midnight
        the symphony is made

Poem of the Midway

Where shall we meet, Marina
Tsvetayeva? Have you any
suggestions for our rendezvous?
And in what year?
I shall clutch a photo of you,

but what of the breath
rising and falling under your
coat, your flush, your rumpled
hair? (You'll run from the station.)
What will you wear?

Somewhere midway. Not in your own
city, Moscow. They stole that
from you. Perhaps in Prague,
the embankment, or the café
full of whores and tears
where your love left you—
yes? (I am jealous.)

Somewhere midway. Or I
will come further, let's say 1950
(aren't lovers prone to
pathetic rushed decisions!) ten
years beyond your death, twenty
behind me now. And not
any street that is likely to
rob me of your whole
joy: you will kiss

more beautifully than any,
and I will love you so fiercely
the wild nerves of your poems
will translate straight into my tongue.
Dress for me with the tremulous
awarenesses of the stripped.
(My hand trembles, shaving.)

Our small talk through our night
together! (We won't sleep.)
I know from your poetry
what you think of God, love,
and your life—that suburb
of a town you're exiled from,
but I want to know your tastes
in wine, clothes, films.

Where shall we meet, Marina
Tsvetayeva? Anywhere in Europe
and our century will be dark
enough for our assignation,
and your poems I'll come holding
will give us enough light
to talk by, across a table.
How cool your hand is.

Kore

Your mouth
is music heard
faintly outside the house
of a maestro

your love
is not in cries or spasms
but in the particular curve
and fluttering movement
of your unseen arms

Blind Girl

Her hand, pitched by the bus's motion,
fell in his lap, and stayed,
moved in his lap, to the bus's rhythm,
while her face
stared ahead
beautiful behind dark glasses.

If the whole earth
was going slowly blind. If the whole earth
tapped through the firmament
on white sticks, white forests of birches.

Healing Spell

as i am nought   my mother
may you be infinite

my rib-cage
enfold you
only as a lantern
its flame

your spirit suck
at my lost milk

at my birth-hour
may you be born

my black tears
form a clear pool
in which waterlilies open

Unnatural Selection

Not daring to look
at the four bloody-faced still-blind
kittens pulling at the tits,
just plunging in my hands
and pulling out three at random
(or almost: the one
I leave, a shade bigger)
to carry off in a cardboard box
to the vet's to be put down.
Their squeaks growing more
and more infrequent.

God is a hardened
mercenary major,
gliding along in plimsolls.

Blue Lake

Picture a man, or a woman,
In a deck-chair, by a blue lake,
Reading a poetry-book.

Suddenly a knee jerks
In surprise at finding
A poem called 'Blue Lake',

About a man, or a woman,
In a deck-chair, by a blue lake,
Reading a poetry-book.

Whose knee jerks
In surprise at finding
A poem entitled 'Blue Lake',

Concerning a man, or a woman,
On a white wall, by a blue lake,
Reading a poetry-book.

Whose knee jerks
In amazement, discovering
A poem entitled 'Blue Lake',

Concerning a man, or a woman, or a child,
On a white wall, by a blue lake,
Reading a poetry-book.

Whose knee jerks
In amazement, discovering
A poem entitled 'Grey Lake'.

It concerns a child,
On a white wall, by a grey lake,
Reading a poetry-book.

Whose knee jerks
In recognition, discovering
A poem entitled 'Grey Lake',

Concerning a child,
On a white wall, by a grey lake,
Reading a fishing magazine.

Who sits up straight
In recognition, discovering
A poem entitled 'White Shark'.

It concerns a child,
On a white wall, by a grey sea,
Reading a fishing magazine.

Who sits up straight
In illumination, discovering
A poem entitled 'White Shark',

Which concerns a child,
On a white wall, by a grey sea,
Dreaming of a white shark,

Which never sleeps, would slash
Its own gut if it could turn
Sharp enough, which dreams

Continuously it is a man, or a woman,
In a deck-chair, by a blue lake,
Reading a poetry-book.

Viking Grave, Greenland

Stop and be moved by
our simple, spare
logistic of death.

This child I held
longer than breath
has crumbled,
and his skeleton
overlaps my own,
wristbone by rib bone.

Wooden cross between
us and this taller
one who leans
slightly away,

to concentrate,
as our wake lessens,
on steering straight
for the polar day,
the midnight sun.

Marriage of Venice to the Sea
on Ascension Day

Note: Gaspara Stampa (1523–54) wrote her most intense
love-sonnets not long before her death, and in the year of
Titian's Danaë and the Golden Shower. One of the sonnets,
which lament her lover's desertion, concludes: 'He in whom
I find new perfections, As a trained eye finds out new stars.'

1

Gaspara Stampa on the Bridge of Sighs.
No feeling surfaces to her cold form
That she is tortured by this meeting-place.
A hand, bloodied by nails, has drawn across

Light a rich scumble of unclearable cloud,
A golden excrement. Her god had come,
Walked on her waters; rises, vanishes.
His gold ring plunges through immensities

Into the canal whose hymen breaks.
She is left by what she is left with: love.
The artist breaks and re-sets; breaks and re-sets,
Shivering like a chain of gondolas;

From his corruption new perfections rising
To her, as a trained eye finds out new stars.

2

Till choice and chosen are suggested there,
The artist breaks, re-sets, breaks and re-sets
Her arm bent on the linen, troubling his sleep.
In excremental gold the god has come.

Now it is finished save the masterstrokes.
His gold ring plunges through immensities;
With his fingers only he perfects
The hand between her thighs, and draws across

Her upturned gaze the limits of creation.
The hymen is broken and the waters break,
The god-child breasts the breakers. He cleans his hands,

And his trained eye already finds new stars.
He turns the imperfect canvas to the wall,
Where she will find, in darkness now, his love.

3

The Bridge of Teats receives the water-Christ's
Benediction. Greeting the holy form,
In the film of sweat that glistens on her breasts
Each whore has traced with scarlet nail a cross.

Jesus the sun amidst white neophytes.
In golden vesture their God has come,
His gaze fixed high above San Marco's lion
As a god's vision might find out new stars.

The crowds fall to their knees. San Marco booms.
He walks the waters, rises, vanishes.
They jostle, embrace. They have seen the groom's
Gold ring flying through immensities.

The Doge puts out to sea. Gold fetors rising
Light a rich scumble of reflective cloud.

4

The lion interrupts with wilder, blue
Light the rich scumble of reflective cloud.
It is high afternoon of the young summer.
Stone walks the waters, water springs from stone.

All delight seems streaming into the city,
To celebrate a tremulous meeting-place.
Action and passion, energy and peace;
Ancient fountains free a hardening form.

Into a glazed lagoon a whore has pissed
A golden excrement. No god has come
With greater ecstasy than her affected

Shivers. Lying back in the gondola,
She takes by chance the image of Danaë,
Warm flesh-tones leaning on a bridge of sighs.

5

They rest, on the Adriatic's bluest skin,
To celebrate a tremulous meeting-place.
The cardinal prays that marriage make them dearer
As a trained eye finds out new stars.

Trumpets. The Doge opens the silver casket.
The hymen is broken and the water breaks.
Under the resettled iconostasis
A gold ring plunges through immensities.

The Doge is moved. He is that mirage
Which walks the waters, rises, vanishes.
Flambeaux flame on the galleys, augment with hymen-
Light the burnt scumble of reflective cloud

Which in the choppier waters, as dusk settles,
An artist breaks, re-sets; breaks, re-sets.

6

He must, must break his custom. Turns to him
The smiling nude. Draws a sharp breath; and sighs:
Seeing the universe concentrated where
A warm canal, beneath the illusioned form,

Secretes the shower her servant cannot catch,
And comes, with ripples like a gondola's.
Yet he, the maker's maker, cannot lie
To consummate a tremulous meeting-place,

Until reality and shadows mix
And into paint his blood is drawn across.
His old hand trembles, touches her shadowy hollow

From whose miasma new perfections rise,
As though his finger could slide in with god.
His gold ring plunges through immensities.

7

The Doge is crying. He has seen his death
Touching his life, a lovers' meeting-place,
In Titian's portrait. He smiled and gave the gold,
But shuddered. Now the chain of gondolas

Turns from the Grand Canal into his death.
The hymen is broken and the waters break.
His gondolier negotiates a canal
Unexpected, tight, like the cleft cut by love

In time's unyielding stone embattlements.
From its miasma new perfections rise
Solacing his heart. A phantom leans.
Her hand, dyked by its blood, is drawing a cross

Over her heart's decision of solitude,
As a trained eye finds out new stars.

8

A high wind blows in salt to her cloaked face.
Night's hymen's broken, her reflection breaks
Under her. A cannon's boom. Carnival shouts.
The rising flood becomes the meeting-place

Of fireflies and contagion. From her despair,
A phrase. Out of it new perfections rise.
A sonnet begins to live. From the wide sea,
Images, like the Doge's gondolas,

Negotiate into lagoons, canals.
The whole world's waters move through a cold form.
Most flows away again. Poetry's stone

Walks on the waters, rises, vanishes.
Even the flowing out she gathers in,
Building out of all loss a Venice, love.

Poem in a Strange Language

Starlings, the burnable stages of stars,
Fall back to earth, lightly. And stars,
Propulsars of angels, die in a swift burn.
And half the angels have fallen below the horizon.

And, falling like alpha particles,
Re-charge the drowned woman
Floating in the bitter lake,
Her hair gold as their blood, her face amazed.

She is Lot's wife, her naked body
Sustained by the salt she has loosened from,
And as her eyes open, grain
Turns green-golden on the black earth of Sodom.

I enter your poem, Mandelstam, yours, Anna
Akhmatova, as I enter my love—
Without understanding anything
Except its beauty and law.

And the way its cloud of small
Movements lifts lightly the fruit
Of a painful harvest and moves
With singing vowels away from death.

III

Love Song on Sand Dunes

Hovering on that consummate shell
Washed from the sea, I hear it say
'This is the true, the holy well,
Crystal and incorruptible.'
The sand has blown the wind away.

'Brush the grains as delicately
From this dark-clear parable,
Creases of a trustful smile,
As from the buried hermit's cell.'
The sand has blown the wind away.

All day there rings a warning-bell,
Or marriage-bell under the sea.
Under the white and trickling hill
We learn each other speechlessly.
The sand has blown the wind away.

Our coupled footprints crumble and fill
All down the lea side of this wall
Against the chill expedient sea;
And we shall never break the spell.
The sand has blown the wind away.

Changeling

Out of the mindless flood, my daughter,
You step into stone circles, pain, laughter.
And I give my promise
Never to recognise
You, meeting you on the moonlit edge of flotsam;
Your eyes will slide from me, not knowing who I am.

Your earth-father, strong as an angel,
Guards your soul and fontanel.
And I, but as the dark's sleight
Of hand that with a weight
of so-light phosphorescence
Touches the sea in silence.

You will haunt my seven ages,
Ghost of the starry images;
Seventh sister of the Pleiades
You will be young when all else fades,
Entwining wildness and purpose,
The cross and the rose.

I will bear you, though you will not know,
Bear your real shadow
Altering my lyre's variations and theme as
A cleaver of windless seas
Senses only by his heart's gauge
The weightless stowaway, the refuge.

You who are dead to me
Will learn speech in my home;
In the dune-chapel of your first communion
Scan the bay for shadowing seal or sea-lion;
I shall bless your wedding-ring
With a gift that is nothing and has no ending.

Kerenza at the Zawn

I don't know where I'm standing;
You say it's a zawn,
We're at the sharp point of the cliff slice
Where the killas has been eaten.

Purposelessly blind, I won't believe
That our love is in danger,
You always threatening
To escape like whirring tyres settling deeper.

Your hand's rubbed smoother by mine, and your cons,
Than the polished boulders in the zawn's turbulence
Till they're no good for anyone else
To hold or enter.

You say the sun is about to set on the sea
Glaring through clouds, a red planet.
I know if we turned to the moor at this instant
A clodgy yellow moon begins to clear

Into clear air.

After a Party

Vaguely the chink of ice
In glasses, the chuckling innuendo of a throng,
Drum-beat, reed-wail. He was the branch tapping the window,
Snowflurry and cablesong,
Husk beneath the ice.

Dead drunk, he knew himself carried up the stairs,
His arms slung round the necks of the two women
Like the two thieves Christ had forgiven.
He gave his jolted sack into their care,
Cataleptic, dead loss. Their albatross.

Grunting, collapsed, they pitched him onto the bed,
A crack of skull on the wall and his eyes glazed
Open. They agreed that he was dead.
Kerenza stripped his shirt only, in tact. Crossed
Their flushed desperate faces then

The lizard snicker of conspirators;
Kerenza fetched a razor and shaving-bowl,
Lowena, a roll of tape,
Sponge, bowl of water, and cottonwool.
The laying-out divided hers and hers.

Lowena has poisoned him with curare,
Saving him from the sea-whore
By grain upon tiny grain, paralysing
His nerve; Kerenza has pulled him from the land-wife,
Drowned him, and dragged him ashore.

Each bent in sorrow and jealousy where
He had turned the obverse face to their love.
Black hair brushed his loins; yellow, his face,
In ritual soixante-neuf,
Sisters' embrace.

Lowena's fingers sealed the anus,
Kerenza's weighted down the lids

With coins; spoke to each other through
His spine; the mouth was taped; his penis to
His thighs; nostrils and ears plugged. Janus,

As the new year struck unheard, tasting
Seeped blood from a razor-nick,
Felt the blade's sting
Against his groin, real death thickening
Over him like an oilslick;

Looked in upon himself, all exits manned,
And tried to cry in that dark for love and joy.
Master of entrances, now all were closed.
Neither could ask him to raise this hand
Or this. His one face smiled, and grew composed.

Friday Evening

You are on the train crawling across country towards me.
I am in the car driving to a half-way station.
You are switching on the overhead reading-light.
I am switching on the car sidelights.
You are losing yourself in a book.
I am losing myself in a poem.
I know this road like the palm of your hand.
To give up is as desperate as to go on.
You lean your head on the glass, speckling with rain like sperm.
I switch on the wipers.
Dusk deepens.
The station will always be there to meet us,
Unable to go even when the last train is in,
Even when the sun flickers low, a waiting-room fire.

Nightride

Clairvoyants are hurling in thousands
their tiny bodies against our windscreen.

We have headaches; I switch on
the wipers, splash up some water.

Catlights hypnotise my headlights
round hairpin bends and adjustments.

Clairvoyants are hurling in thousands
their tiny bodies against our windscreen

and somewhere beyond their amazing splats
against 70 mph reinforced glass,

behind our car,
the small gnats and flies wing on
where their deaths have not yet hit them.

Euridice

This death
Is a declaration of independence.
I wait
In the closed room of her corpse
Which glistens and breathes, uncorrupted.
With the flare and smoke of my endless cigarettes
I could have travelled a long journey.
I have travelled a long journey.
Is it, as in a train,
I who am dead
And she, in agony, trying to draw me alive?

Can I make love to you, Euridice?
Not expecting you to move a muscle?
Necrophilia appals you.
Can I masturbate in sight of your body?
Love degrades more than death.

And once, I said to her corpse, promise me
If you feel the least stirring of life
You will move your hand, you will touch me,
If only my hand; and I will not touch you
But only allow whatever you wish to happen.
And I believe that her hand touched
My side, and it said, how thin you have grown,
And it stroked my side. And the dead hand stroked
My thighs and moved up, slowly, and her nipples
Were flowering, and I hoped that she wished
Me to enter her, and I did.
But she is dead, dead.

And when she said, I can see a glimmer of hope,
There was a star,
But her death has so confused all logic,
I could not see if it belonged to any constellation,
Behind the clouds of her eyes.
And looking at the star too intently
I covered it in darkness.

Surgery

She is the doctor of verities.

She says to the woman, You must leave him who is your love
and your life, or you will not live.
Here is valium.
It will take you on a train journey
but it will lead only to a station
late at night, that knows only two directions,
the asylum, and a street without addresses.

She says to the man, You must leave her you do not love
even though love says you cannot.
Here is librium.
It will take you on a plane-flight,
but at its grounding your love and your love
will arrive together like cases on the revolving track,
both full of almost identical woman's things,
one with so many articles of you, and so many children's,
and you must pick up one. It is impossible any more
to pick up both. One must go on revolving
and you must walk away.
And she writes, for the woman and for the man,
separately,
prescriptions in a language
she herself hardly begins to know.

Something to carry her into the terrible valley.
Something to carry him into his terrible liberation.

She does not know what kind of whole
she is asking them to fall into.
She trembles.
Her own issue of blood
wanting to touch some god's garment.

The Blue Shift

High over
Washington
she loses
her strained smile.
'Do not smoke,'
she tells us,
'while breathing
oxygen.'
Then whispers
for no-one
but the clouds,
'Nor suckle
your child while
aborting.'

She carries
her own bomb.
I watch her
skull broken
constantly
in hundreds
of thousands
of jigsaw
fragments, blank
and white as
Labrador.
But she re-
constitutes.

Her bones are
churned up by
many ploughs,
she becomes
cirrus-cloud,
madonna
of the rocks,
of cocktails,
but mostly

that pure blue,
her home is
never here.

More and more
stars gather
in the sky,
too many
prodigal
suns, streaming
home, over
too many
fields of time,
to be fed
by Lucy.

She, the blue
stewardess,
has taken
control and
turned the craft
back into
the dawn, the
darkness, to
head for her
own country.

Our journey
shadows time,
I can see
the watch-hands,
luminous,
of the blue
stewardess,
always at
six o'clock.

Her breath is
warm, comforts.
She shakes me
for the dawns

that never
come, keeping
me going
through black days.

The sound of
a river
beside us.
Once, in her
camera-
flash, the leap
of a fish.

Suddenly,
after days
of dark flight,
the white breasts
of mountains
loom at us.

Where was a
house, faces,
at space's
edge, nothing
can haunt it.

She weeps for
nothing but
a child's shoe
by a well.

Light flies back
to the blue
stewardess.

She rides forth,
armed, erect,

dead, victrix.

Stands at the
bay in red.

You Are On Some Road

The evening star
trembling in blue light

The red star
breaking through the dusk
like acetylene

The Orion stars
blossoming
like desert flowers

Even the pleiads
sharply visible
like children in white
on a dark street

Tribes of stars
never seen before
drumming beyond the drift
of the Coal Sack

You are on some road

IV

Sonoran Poems

I descend I enter you
a diplomat sick of negotiations
choosing to be hijacked
by a blue stewardess
with a gun instead of champagne

in the midst of a ghost-town
in the midst of a desert
to rest
to forget time and the six
directions to be forgotten

I have sheets of paper
a typewriter
the clean necessities

How peaceful to forget
all diplomacy all ruinous compromises
impossible settlements

warring ideologies
sitting down at table with me
children always the stumbling block
their hearts like ricebowls

I have seen secretaries
leave the too-crowded city streets
to enter the expensive clinic
passing foetuses in the revolving doors

I have stumbled over their parts

Give me the harsh command
be with me or die

Life is an aristocrat
the poor are crowding behind the stars
clutching roots under the desert
the remotest part of any verb is
if they should have been loved

This tarantula
came green and secret
in the great clusters of hot sunlight
survives the Sonoran cold
by inertia
its furred and muscletensioned legs contemplate
its brain serenely

I
in a strange heat
begin to move

How beautiful
the crackle of white sheets
in the desert

Yet fearful
to be in the hands of extremists
a mouth of pure dialectic
from which shit falls every ten seconds

In our first coming together
your finger probes my anus
is this love
or do you seek
my breaking-point and identity

Sonoran
let me first find myself
in the mid-cipher of your cloudless name

Are you my enemy
or my only friend   fire-girl of Sonoran
unlike the Catalinas
death may be closer than I think

but I think in these four days
I have crossed the great waters
I have seen my father above the sun

I walk out of my life
as from a conference

Perhaps I shall root here like the saguaros
root with their long but shallow roots

Through the judas hole you have made me
october red stars move breathlessly close

Stand under the porch lantern-light
bringing as a love gift
in your long and straight hair
bewildering stars of the Sonoran
at the expiration of this spell

Like a kachina-mask
you wear your beauty like a kachina-mask
        your beauty

the minute you are gone
        desert rain
            red
            mariposa lilies
            astonished
            mariposa lilies

From desert scrub the lord's candles glimmer
a wind shivers and I am changed

without knowing it yet
without holding it yet
mistaking it for joy

I become good
I become loyal to myself

moment by moment
new stars made

O Mother of Tonantsin
O Our Lady of Guadalupe

You wake me like a ghost-town

In our smiles' poker-games
harlots disguised as hostesses

a posse of shutters watches
which breath will draw faster

even the sun instantly
has dipped from sight

I have never known
such silence
in this road

Pale paloverde trees
dig us the one grave

The bulblight flickers
figures are there searching
combing the ghost-town

You stand with blue lips
back to the door
alien and fanatic
covering me

But how can love recede
but how can love recede
those slit domes
through which the night keeps pouring

These are the five days
outside the calendar

The first is Hair
high noon and desert starlight convocate

The second is Eye
a day of mourning a quetzal-
plumed aztec chief vanishing into the sun's black target

The third is Hand
strangely small and muted and undramatic
aligned to my mood of observing things

The fourth is Soul
it is tomorrow

The fifth is Vagina
after the storm I go out into its silence
and find fresh paloverde trees and my dream-song

It is my kachina-mask
it is my kachina-mask
instead of patched jeans
you come to me dressed
as the traditional spy
and seducer quelling your nature
it is my birthday you say

long black gloves
garterbelt and stockings
tense as a strung bow

I fuck it as I pretend
it is you I fuck
it is the fetich I fuck
it is the god
the mountain around which
everything moves it is here
and here and here
in these fulcra of greatest anguish

I adore the oppugnant stresses
agent and double agent and triple agent

wearing my kachina-mask
I will betray anything
wearing my kachina-mask

You
the song
bring a smile to my lips
I cannot silence

Muse you are dead
why do you walk along my dreams
my dry veins
hunting your murdered children
and wailing and scratching huge rents
in the backs of lost travellers
like the ghost-woman of the sandflats of the Santa Cruz

Houses are nets of intrigue
poisonous diaries at nightfall
bedrooms plotting against dressing-rooms
dressing-rooms against guest-rooms
guest-rooms against studies
studies against drawing rooms

burning jealousy and shivering excitement
pressing scorches on the same breasts

all arteries by love corrupted

shall I betray its treachery

Now as the earth curves gently like her lying breast
    now our days ring with each other's sleep

I am tired of faces
that shine next to me as close
as a filling station the other side a motorway
softly shining
at night

You have braided this delicate braid
because I would like it

your confession is a drunk tractor-driver
veering and singing for joy in a prairie of corn
between Mexican silver and Arizonac gold

Let the downpour be stored

Stars of the Sonoran
be jealous of her hair
descend still closer
and blind to its radiance
whom she is with

Hair of my new love
of my extremist
dim the close stars
that who walks with her
receive no power

Night
and through the judas hole
one blue star
questions my meaning

Blue star
I do not intend
to hide or escape
let them do their worst

Let her who is fated
hold a gun to my head
with shaking fingers
prepared to kill

A woman you become
time and again
blue star
a woman you become

Which of them blue
star are you by whom
through the judas hole
I am truly seen

You
the song
I
the dream

In beauty it is finished

The white wind blows by day
the blue wind all the time
the white wind masks the blue
the blue wind blows all the same
at night the white wind dies
the blue wind is supreme

If ever the blue wind die
it will take the form of a song
sacred in every note
it will not ever be heard
everything will be there
it will be so short a song

My soul is very lonely
blind he has touched your face
he sends me to be a go-between
to beg you to come

bring a flower of the saguaro cactus
to cure my friend

The indian cemetery at Xan Xavier
square and facing east
their white and nameless crosses

your hand gently enchaining me
and your eyes with love releasing me
it is not of death I think
on this happy day
but as if the whole universe moves towards the east

Notes to the poems: 'kachina' (Pueblo-Navajo)—any form
concealing a god's presence; 'the lord's candles'—yucca
blossoms; 'saguaros' (pronounced Su-aro)—tall, limbed
cactuses.

V

Lilith

This is she who stands behind the world
As eyes behind a bough.
She watches as the blood of Arab or Jew,
Terrorist, avenger, spurts; her menstrual shame
Still pouring through.
The cuntjuice God, then Adam, then Satan, stirred
Still falls as dew.
Strands of her hair she combed to still her shudders
Still tosses as grain.
The one tear that slithered from her eyelid
Still drums as rain.
The one song she is known to have sung
Beethoven and Mozart looked for in vain.
Attitude, colour, as she squatted and pissed
Tormented Rodin
And weighed with slime
The blinding palettes of the impressionists.

Lilith-prints

Satan shoves
his phallus into kneeling Lilith,
the first sabbath, her mouth
split like a birth-channel loves

God's to orgasm.
Satan fills her as death
fills slowly Adam's last breath
and translates his spasm

to Belsen, cancer, Hiroshima,
children's screams
taperecorded. Instantly

God's trickling semen
starts love's endless creative dreams,
angels guarding the sleepers, endlessly.

God half fills
Lilith supine. Is it farce
or divine comedy? The stars
merely shine. Nothing spills

from the milky nebula,
nothing says
that his stroke withdraws
or enters the vagina

more deeply still.
The print
murders all motion,

clouding their faces' real
or apparent
emotion.

God taking
the still at evening fresh
waters of her apricot-lush
tongue, Adam slaking

a different, urolagnic thirst.
Roused by the lubricity
of his magnetic lingus she
lets other waters burst

for him: a murkier wine,
a misty cider harvest
from carboned trees,

a sewer-cycled rain,
cloacal feast,
stupendous lees.

Eve halfclad blonde
Lilith naked and dark,
the birch's silver bark
by the blind desolate pond,

Lilith's ringed finger as a birch
cool, enters Adam's anus,
ring round ring round ring of pain as
the gliding search

goes on, and the foiled
phallus groans in the grip
of Eve's free

hand, her Orion belt coiled
like a snake or moebius strip
round her, into eternity.

God crepitates
a violent crack
to Lilith's tongue, gives back-
word, creates

a hurricane
of energy,
poetry,
flattens the Troy plain

against the twentieth century's power-
house, whose blast
fading starts a shock-

wave, a krakatoa
still makes us hold fast.
Blok.

Crucifixed Lilith alone,
hands joined in the Mayan jungle
temple of her beaded tangle,
her gaze a candid dome,

mountain telescope
starlight seeps
or cold sunlight steeps
a dazzling heliotrope,

white hands cupped in prayer,
copula & cupola, nun. None
need return for centuries,

still every galaxy's
curved invisible burn
is printed there.

Grand Canyon
and Siberian meteorite,
black light
and neon,

Lilith and God
locked in copulation and
her licentious hand
rests on the limp rod

of Adam. Dries
on Lilith's belly, God's scrotum,
his come, lachrymae christi,

on Lilith's wild face the dyes
run, post coitum
omne animal triste.

The dream on Lilith's closed
eyes, over Adam's shoulder
or God's, makes it clear
that of the army, the host,

her joyful throes
gave out, one
snowblind napoleon
survives the retreat, the snows,

has returned.
Into quarrystone
she is ready to burst,

to have each stone ground
into atoms of a universe
to be created by her son.

Lilith kneels, a dog
straddles her hips,
at her ear the lips
and eloquent tongue of God.

All storm and calm
resonates in that shell,
thrill upon thrill
vibrates the exquisite drum.

Spurt upon spurt,
minotaur spasms,
floods the under-palace,

at Lilith's heart,
the scallop-shell, the maze,
flutters the orgasm.

Commerce of breasts,
tongues, genitals,
steam falls
into mingled rainforests.

Eve's eyes
atone,
streams running over stones
they refract her certainties,

radiate into a capital
achieved in hillier
solitudes, a condor

city. Blinded by candor
and design, her brow's Brazilia,
—back, back the jungles fall.

God makes her. Brow
to instep Eve blossoms round
the nothing he imagined
shaped to his tool. Now

this all his phallus
held, holds all his gaze,
the central nothing dies.
A palace,

a more than Taj
Mahal, to house a bride's tomb
commanded by despair;

round the pearled central room
such joyous architecture flowers, the Raj
orders the tomb elsewhere.

Lilith blows
her mind and arse,
laughs when he wears
her clothes,

and laughs
when he sniffs, fingers and thumb,
strontium, oil and opium
from her three shafts.

In nothing
is Lilith shy,
nothing she will not encompass

for a king
who has built a palace
upon a privy.

Lilith depilated,
except for these
unuprootable trees
of juju, infested

with brigands,
dragons.
Cached flagons,
weapons,

lurk, cark,
below obscene roots,
a scritchowl flutters,

hoots,
ventriloquial, dark,
guerillas, woodcutters.

God fucking Lilith
makes days and nights. Satan
added, makes seasons.
Eve added, makes death

and life. The stars
flash into their places,
slow to a rhythm. Moonphases
begin as Lilith's curse

trickles behind God's
stabbing thrusts. Adam
added, makes the poles

of blue and red
shifts, sudden
withdrawals make black holes.

Words, obscenities,
he thinks of, whispers
to her passivity, STARS,
WIND, GALAXIES,

and vagina and mouth
delightedly hollow
into caves, swallow
more hungrily, and Lilith

gives back whisper,
creation no longer dreams
in God's skull, but is, blazes,

as a revved accelerator
raises
interior light and fading beams.

Candaules-
God, so much worships
Lilith's capacious hips,
wants to be jealous,

not to have her, all,
sites Gyges-Satan
behind a curtain
of lightspeed, where galaxies fall

into nothing. But Lilith, as
she is meant, sees
his erection's silhouette,

and dreams too much
of him, needs his touch,
his seed. Cannot forget.

Poem from the Book of Changes

Their blood
pounding, they wait
by a
trembling footbridge over
the swollen stream
for the midwife.

Through the black
night the mountain
is being flushed
by its
own placenta into
their glen.

He is born
to be
embalmed by
those fluttering hands,
the scentless scent
of leaves.

She is
born to
sink, a
slender moon,
into a marsh
of pleased satisfaction.

Her breast
is full.
She gathers
all she
loves into an
attic room.

Parched, they drink
each other,
from a
single glass
clouded with the
fallout of mountains.

Not snow,
but wind
through the
branches. She holds
her white
skirt down.

Her so
pliable limbs
are singing like
cherry branches
overwhelmed by
the wind.

She gashes open,
tangy, moist,
a great
fruit that
has not
been eaten.

He is mounted.
The whole earth
beyond horizons is
his. Blue haze
of distance charms
his tenant's house.

She wears
a yellow
shift like
an orchard.
She treads
on hoarfrost.

Thunder is
felt through
floor and soles.
The white fence
is entangled in
a ram's horns.

How young
she is, how
wideapart are her
legs! A marsh
is holding a
flowering willowtree.

Her thighs,
his thighs, her
hands again
in the
centre. It is
all flowing.

Or his thighs,
her thighs,
his hands again
in the centre.
It is
all clinging brightness.

She becomes
the muscle of
the calf. He
becomes the springing
movement of
the foot.

He lies
under her.
The grass
she plucks may
bring with it
the whole earth.

He slides over
her. Her hands
unclenched and helpless
are stained
with grass
and earth.

He treads squeamishly
through pools of
shit. His eyes,
she sees,
are the dry
crust of dung.

She trails
her empty
basket home. She
has eaten
the berries meant
for the boilingpan.

Gentle penetration restores
their closeness. He
moves as
though his lust
is a mouth
just breathing.

Her teeth form
a misty crescent.
Cautiously she
is peering
out of
the door.

The rich sun,
the motherly
king, has appeared
to her
from behind
a mountain.

Granaries are being
dispersed to the
poor. He
swims without
effort, insulated
in shining grease.

A messenger
from the
uncertain field he
is beginning to
pace himself. The
sun explodes.

He must climb
away. The hot
glaciers are simply
the foothills of
the mountains
of air.

His mouth cannot
impose his
will. He is
a talking
traveller in a
carriage of ghosts.

He moves awkwardly
and rests.
A large wagon
with its wealth
circled by its
five dimmed fires.

Grass into meat.
The sweet
grass on which
he lies has
to digest too
much death.

And she
freezes. They are
clock-hands
stopped at noon
or midnight,
someone dying.

Thunder. Rain.
Her falling
pulse-beat is
in the
hands of a
carbon clock.

Tears splash on
the hot iron.
The hot
iron scorches silk.
Silk dabs
at tears.

Arms, legs and
hands, he
contains her
absolutely in
stillness. He is
her oak coffin.

There is a
small movement of
hands. They
are making
a coffin
into a boat.

She is
water gathered into
one place, above
the earth,
and walled
against dissipation.

Life is
being drawn even
from the
wells to which
the birds no
longer come.

Caresses by
the mild tiger
at his shoulder
are changing all
the skin
of his body.

Her breath
growing faster,
she is
a village girl
ascending into a
great city.

She recalls
their son,
benighted somewhere far
off, very
near. Thunder-
stroke after stroke.

Mountain above mountain.
Her sighing
throat is
a receiver blocked
from all
radio waves.

Wild geese are
gradually approaching land.
The tree
where they will
rest is
swiftly growing.

The sun's eclipse
is slowing
in the
sky for
the cover of
the moon's eclipse.

He is
so screened
from the midday
sun he can
see the plough's
ghostly impression.

Her body gleams,
pearly. Her
jewellery-box
is open. She
is not
a collapsing star.

Rather than scream,
their love
bites on whatever
is the
hardest thing
they can find.

His head
tilts back. It
is getting dark.
He must
enter his
house and rest.

Their bodies have
drowned together. Across
a wind-
shaken lake
he is rowing
an empty boat.

The crane
cries out
for her young.
How can she
dare to
soar higher?

Vagina becomes
mouth, wet hair
becomes eyes,
womb becomes mind,
her mind
becomes the sky.

Wet from head
to tail,
a young fox,
a red
salmon, is crossing
the river.